MINE THE MINE

MINE THE MINE

by Divine Emole

Published independently by
Divine Emole and designed by Victor Okpara

Dedication

To all individuals who are actively engaged in creating and developing innovative solutions, regardless of age, as they use their minds to produce beautiful content, models, software applications, and more that benefit our world. In a world where people often prefer to avoid processes that require effort and attention to detail, your work is particularly valuable.

To my two brilliant boys, Charisma and Doxazo, and the myriad of brilliant minds who are currently exploring the depths of their thoughts, destined to make a significant impact on the world and become creators of great institutions. Your minds have the potential to generate innovate solutions even if you have yet to be recognized by the world.

Acknowledgment

This piece of work is product of the collective effort of many brilliant minds. I am forever grateful for the inspiration and wisdom imparted by the numerous great teachers and mentors, men and women, who have passionately contributed to my growth, and enriched the content of this work.

My heartfelt appreciation goes to my ever-supportive wife, Bliss, and our children for their unwavering patience, understanding, and contribution during my busy schedules and engagements outside the home. Your unwavering support makes it easy for me to fulfill divine purpose.

I must also recognize the exceptional production team behind this book. The literary prowess and editing skills of Somadina James, together with the beautiful layout and cover design by Victor Okpara have undoubtedly elevated this work to a class of its own.

Finally, to THE GREATEST MIND THERE IS AND EVER WILL BE, the source and supplier of all potential, the Omnipotent One, the Father and Lord of all creation; His Son, my Saviour, Jesus Christ; and my personal Counselor, The Holy Spirit. Thank You, Lord for the privilege of serving you.

Inside this Book

Introduction

A Secret Not So Secret

Over the years, attempts have been made by great philosophers and psychologists to explain man. Some have said that he is a creature of circumstances; some others have argued that man is a creature of habits. While it may seem really smart to say that man is a creature of circumstances such as that which causes the birth of a baby to happen; it is important to also see that man has control over circumstances; as Benjamin Disreali would say, "Man is more than the matter." Man is neither a creature of circumstances nor of habit; man is a creature of the predominant factor that produces his habits—thoughts. Man is a product of his thoughts. So, the renowned Jewish King Solomon put it this way, "as a man thinketh, so is he." It's the thoughts of a man that makes the man. So without a distinct thought pattern, he is "a man"; he only becomes "The man" as a reflex of his most dominant thoughts.

I have seen a great truth during my time here on the ball. A man no matter how well behaved, holy, spiritual, and ungodly, lives out the reality of where he has been in thoughts. So, a man can be very spiritual and still have a very unattractive life because the quality of a man's life is determined by the quality of his mind.

Many times, the church of Jesus Christ has believed that the revival comes every time to urge her away from mental exploits. It has been widely believed that the job of the church here is nothing other than to pray and preach. A very subtle lie has been told to many of God's people.

In this book, I show you a secret not so secret; God's gift to man, the ability to create his possibilities by the mere act of thinking. Come along with me as we explore this inexhaustible mine of wealth lying deep within the clay called man.

Chapter One

> ***"The mind is never idle; it is either building up or tearing down."***

The Mine Material

I made up my mind not too long ago that when sharing some truths, I will openly inform my audience that a certain truth that I am about to share is for believers only. This is because not everyone believes and for the unbeliever, spiritual truths make no sense. Transformation and progress all happen in the mind. It is through mental reformation that man experiences transformation. A degenerate mind can't discern the goodness of the good news or even the will of God because the carnal mind cannot process spiritual things. The mind is never idle; it is either building up or tearing down. Paul tells us that it is by being transformed that we will not be conformed to the world. It is by the renewing of your mind. Renewal is a one-time thing. Renewing however is a continuous occurrence. Nobody proves anything without thinking. The above scripture does not in any way suggest that the will of God is three-folded. It is saying that once proved, the will of God always comes out to be good, acceptable, and perfect. I've heard preachers talk of a "permissive will of God" but in truth, there is no such thing. Jesus praying in Gethsemane said to The Father;

And he said, Abba, Father, all things are possible unto thee; take away this cup from me: nevertheless not what I will, but what thou wilt. Mark 14:36

I like the way The Passion Translation and New Living Translation puts the text in Romans 12:2

Do not copy the behavior and customs of this world, but let God transform you into a new person by changing the way you think. Then you will learn to know God's will for you, which is good and pleasing and perfect. NLT

Stop imitating the ideals and opinions of the culture around you, but be inwardly transformed by the Holy Spirit through a total reformation of how you think. This will empower you to discern God's will as you live a beautiful life, satisfying and perfect in his eyes. TPT

Our lives are altered to the degree to which we alter our thoughts. Until a man is changed in his mind, he cannot truly change. The man is his mind. Pick a madman on the street, get him to get a nice haircut, and get him clothes and shoes from the best designers. All you need to do is let him out of your sight for a few minutes and you'll realize just how much change you've done to him. Outward change is a product of inward transformation. No man can rise above the level of his thoughts. Even when a person changes their environment, it only takes a while before his environment starts to look like his thoughts. You are as powerful as the way you think.

Whether a man succeeds or fails, rises or falls, is a function of his thoughts. A man's life will always gravitate in the direction of his most dominant thoughts.

For as he thinketh in his heart, so is he........ -Pro 23:7

Permit me to also add that **as a man continues to think, so does he continue to be.** Mental renewal is one of the hardest duties of the Holy Ghost in a believer's life. Man is a spirit; he has a soul which is the passageway from his spirit to his body. At new birth, our spirits get changed instantly; our bodies will be instantly changed at the return of the Lord. The only part of man that takes a while to experience transformation is the mind. This is why it is important to mind what you listen to because the mind works only within the boundaries of the information available to it. Faith comes by hearing; it goes through our minds into our spirits to give us energy. It is necessary to pay attention to what we listen to, especially for those in third-world countries because our limitations are functions of our mental programming and not functions of our environments. Our results and lives are products of our mental conditioning. It has been sold to many people in developing nations that life is hard, and that it is impossible to escape the prevalent hardships in their home countries. The truth remains that in these same countries, prosperous business and career people are thriving at what they do, regardless of the overarching deficiencies in confidence.

As believers, we believe to live. The just it is written, shall live by faith. Whatever the heart ponders on for too long, it believes. And what it believes, the man becomes. Your limitations are there because your mind puts them. I feel very bad when I see people living in envy. To be envious is to declare oneself an unqualified candidate for success; so envious people take it upon themselves to attack the successful. The problem is with our imaginations; so, Paul admonished us to cast down imaginations and everything that exalts itself against the knowledge of Christ.

Certain restricting beliefs have over the years kept Christians stagnant and immobile in the area of their callings and careers; they were told that making more money would affect their relationships with their Lord. So, they avoid wealth because according to popular opinion, it's a nemesis. But you'll agree with me that Christianity is better when believers can pay their bills. If only believers will leave popular opinion to follow Bible opinion. Some others believe that they are not progressing because someone from their hometown is doggedly dedicated to making sure that they don't progress. Here is the gist; nobody is against your progress. That tag is an opinion that you have allowed to stay in your mind.

It is also very sickening to see people praying for undeserved promotion in their workplaces, forgetting that it doesn't work that way; God does not promote mediocrity. Of Daniel and his friends, it was said that they were ten times better than their contemporaries in the matter of wisdom and understanding. (See *Daniel 1:20*). So, it's a foolish thing to call the God of Daniel your God and not practice the diligence of Daniel and his friends. The same Daniel was also reported to have been found not wanting in the matters that pertained to the king and the kingdom because an excellent spirit was in him (*Daniel 6:2-4*). Daniel's mind worked so well that he topped the list when it was time for promotion.

The Passion Translation renders Romans 12:2 this way;

"Stop imitating the ideals and opinions of the culture around you, but be inwardly transformed by the Holy Spirit through a total reformation of how you think. This will empower you to discern God's will as you live a beautiful life, satisfying and perfect in his eyes."

For many years, religious people have thought that it's all about praying only and that has resulted in the spread of mediocrity. While praying remains an integral part of our faith, it is important to note that thinking is too. Think as much as you pray. When you pray, ideas and inspiration drop, thinking is the tool for processing that information you receive via revelation. Have a thinking book where you write down all your inspirations, processed and not. There is a highly demonic spirit presently operating in our age; people no longer like to write things down, and there is a present plague of book-laziness. What you'll find notorious in such people is the critical spirit. They turn to referees who watch for faults and loopholes in other people. A focused driver rarely sees distractions.

We see a clear illustration of the power of imagination in the story in Genesis 11:6. Perhaps you may want to take a look at it for yourself:

And the Lord said, Behold, the people is one and they all have one language; and this they begin to do: and now nothing will be restrained from them which they have imagined to do.

The above text shows us that you don't begin anything the moment you put in the first physical or fiscal effort; you begin when you first imagine it. To imagine is to build without laying bricks. To imagine means to create mental images of what you aspire to do in your mind. So, before you sit down to imagine, there should be a purpose. Some people don't even know that families should have visions. So, they go on to start a family without first asking, "What is the family coming to earth to do? Imagination is images in action. There is no restriction to what we can build in our minds. The sad news is that the average man waits for challenges to come before putting their mind to work but the truth is that you don't need challenges to challenge your mind to work.

A foreigner walks into Nigeria with a pair of shorts and a briefcase and after a while, they are employing locals to work for them, while an average Nigerian goes about believing that nothing works here and so, nothing can work for him no matter how hard he tries. The difference between the two people is their minds; the foreigner believes that there are opportunities and so much gold in Nigeria, while the Nigerian thinks as he has been conditioned to think. I remember a protégé of mine some years ago who was making pastries in school. Upon graduation, he put someone in charge of the business while he went for service. At the expiration of his one year-service tenure, he came back and said he was going to get a job; he already had 3 people working for him by the way. I guess you're probably wondering why he'd think of doing that. Well, you guessed right if you blamed the prevalent mental conditioning here before now; those days; the fad was to go job-hunting immediately after service. Before the reality of job scarcity hit the Nigerian youth populace, only very few thought about job creation so many were starting businesses in school only to abandon them upon graduation to go after jobs that will put them in suits and lack. They abandon their businesses to go take up jobs that pay below $200 a month. They'd rather be in suits and earn so little than be in shorts like Mark Zuckerberg and create jobs for the average masses.

God's will for every man is that we are co-creators with Him. When He made man, He said to him, ***be fruitful, and multiply, and replenish the earth, and subdue it; and have dominion*****.....*****Gen 1:28.***

Every man on earth becomes a creator and value-provider as God designed us to be, there still is enough space on earth for houses to be built; the earth is enough. There is enough land. The bitter truth about neglecting this divine principle is that ***"when you refuse to think, you become a slave to the reality of another man's thoughts."***

Have you ever tried to communicate a vision or idea of yours to someone very close to you and they left you sorely discouraged after the conversation? Well, if you've been in a similar situation then you're not alone. You should not blame them, what you should do however is to get yourself away from them because they're speaking from where they are. The fact that you're feeling discouraged by them is a pointer that God has determined a separate path for you. The truth is that ***when God wants to change a man's status and use such man for impact, He separates the man from the environments that sponsor his limiting mindsets.*** In the case of Joseph, God used his sale into slavery as an occasion to orchestrate his transformation; it was an escape away from his brothers who were angry at the disclosure of the young man's dreams because of their overly poor mindsets. Had that not been the case they wouldn't have gotten envious. A better mindset would have let them know that what the young man saw was only his throne, not theirs. Instead of being jealous, they could have gone back to dream their dreams too. They were being irresponsible with their positions so God was determined to set up the responsible one to preserve the seed of Israel. God had to take Joseph out from their midst because ***no one can change a place they think like***. Perhaps this is the confirmation you needed to be sure that the voice you're hearing is genuine. It's time to change your friends; if they don't challenge you, then it's time to change them. If they praise you for mediocrity every time you are with them even when you know you need so much to learn, then it's time to move on if they won't come with you.

The result of this mental transformation is that it gives us the ability to prove what the will of God is; that will is that every man becomes a creator. Be fruitful, multiply, replenish the earth, and have dominion. If everyone on earth can be a value provider, there'll still be enough space on the blue marble earth for people to build whatever they set out to.

There is enough land on earth to go around. The tragedy of refusing to think is that it enslaves you to other people's thoughts; you will serve the reality of another man's thoughts.

You will always be poor if you always think that you're poor. The man is his thoughts. Things will always be difficult if you always think that things are difficult. If you always think of possibilities, even where people call impossible, there will be a way for you.

The day a man takes control of his mind, he will begin to experience new things. Henry Ford, the businessman who founded "Ford Motors" company was quoted to have said, "Whether you think you can or you think you cannot, you are right." If someone says they can't do a thing, it's fine, let them be if they refuse to see that it can be done. If you're a CEO and your employee says that something cannot be done, and you know it can correct them. If after you have tried to improve them and given them a shot at becoming better, they refuse to change, fire them, and feel no remorse about it. Some people would require firing them. Don't build your business on emotions. If after investing time, patience, and effort in a person and they fail to yield profits, disengage from them. We must intentionally break free from thought patterns that do not move our lives forward, and one of the ways to do that is by moving ourselves out from the company of like-minded folks. A pessimist will remain a pessimist as long as he continues to roll with pessimists.

When we pray for God to change our circumstances, we must first learn to change the way we think. ***Prayers are really answered when our prayers agree with our thoughts.*** God can answer your prayers and yet your thoughts will draw you back to where he delivered you from. Change happens first on the inside.

Beloved, I wish above all things that thou mayest prosper and be in good health, even as thy soul prospereth. - III John 2:1

A sick soul will produce a sick body; a sick mind will produce a sick business. You can't be sick in your mind and have a healthy body.

"The mind is the true being, and if the mind is not well, the man is not well. We are not called human doings; we are human beings. We be to do; we don't do to be."

Of the mind, one of my favorite authors, James Allen, said that the mind is a master weaver both of the inner garment of character and the outer garment of circumstances. It is the mind that weaves our circumstances. How does it happen? Whatever you give your mental attention to, you are more likely to become. Whoever comes to the point of controlling his thoughts, can control their lives.

It is said that 5% of the world's population controls the remaining 95%. Why is this? When you ask, some Christians will tell you that it is a divine election. I beg to differ; since I am not trivializing the place of advantages of spirituality; it suggests that there is a level of plain ground that the average person can compete from to reach the top, and that plain ground is the way you think. Your thoughts determine your character; your thoughts after a while, break down into words.

A man communicates based on the depth of his thoughts. It is said in leadership that the first person to lead is not your neighbour; the first person to lead is you. A man that cannot lead himself cannot lead anybody. It is also said that the first organ to master is the mind. ***You can't mine your mind until you have mastered it.*** Everyone thinks, the difference, however, is how often we think, the quality and depth of our thoughts, and the translation of processed thought into accompanying efforts. This is what distinguishes exceptional people from the crowd. How often do you think?

Chapter Two

...it is fellowship that oils your thinking.
God thinks why shouldn't you?

"

The Mine Escavator

Thinking is simply an act of processing information until it becomes usable. Success in life is a product of deliberate steps taken towards the desired end. There is no accidental success; just as we cannot say that a roadside accident was a successful one. Life and success in life must be gone about deliberately. The point of being deliberate can only be achieved by thinking; intentionality is a product of thinking. The difference between any two men is simply the way they think. People that do better and best in any sphere of influence are always those that think; that's the difference between any two people, ministries, organizations, and even families. What differentiates men from the crowd is how and what they think. The way people think determines what they do and that's what makes them stand out from the masses. A man that thinks cannot be part of the masses. The masses are those that depend on the government and not on their mind. I have made up my mind to be exceptional in life but I realized that exceptional living is a product of exceptional thinking. Learn to think beyond the expected if you want to have an exceptional performance; learn to think beyond the bar. People that think this way always set themselves up for recognition. Think beyond the anticipated result.

People often complain about where they are; the best thing to do when you're tired of where you are is not to complain. The best thing to do is to retreat, to think. When was the last time you thought? There is a level of creative thinking that will move you from where you are right now to your next level.

He is able to do exceeding abundantly above all you ask or think... Ephesians 3:20

This scripture places prayer and thinking on the same pedestal. It also merges the effect of the two. It doesn't matter how much you pray; if you don't think, you will still pray. There is a delusion that the devil is selling in our day; this delusion is selling because the church was not presented with the whole truth. I remember my dad telling me about how they sold some lands because they thought Jesus was coming. The church was thought to pray; the church was thought to fellowship, but the church was not thought to think. This is the delusion that the devil is now selling to our generation that our fathers that prayed and fellowshipped a lot didn't achieve much. So the devil proposes to us that the other end is safer; to be more logical and place reasoning above prayer and fellowship. So, today a Christian cherishes his job more than fellowship. Not understanding that ***it is fellowship that oils your thinking.***

He is able to do exceeding abundantly, all you could ask or think, according to the power at work in you....

Take note that it is the spiritual force that dwells in you that makes you think and makes available the power to bring about the reality of your thinking. ***Do not pray without thinking and do not think without praying.***

Because some things will not come by education; some things come to the spirit of man by revelation, but what is given to you by revelation is processed by thinking.

A minstrel that downloads sounds from heaven does not download the partings and arrangements of the sound too; he receives the sound by revelation and then puts his mind to work to make the song fully ready for consumption. I realized that the conscious mind, once activated, drops information for the subconscious; and the subconscious mind is the wellspring of creativity. People pray to God to raise a thinking church; I say, "No, add thinking to your church". Raising a thinking church may bring us a church that will think and not pray.

The weapons of our warfare are not carnal; they are mighty through God, to the pulling down of strongholds.....

We use might through God to organize our thoughts. Times, when you find yourself in a state of quagmire or dilemma, are not times to complain; they are times to retreat and think.

As the heavens are above the earth, so are my thoughts higher than your thoughts.....

God thinks why shouldn't you?

Clothes, houses, fridges, air conditioners, and everything that makes life beautiful are products of thought. Thinking is what creates; it is through thinking that some things are birthed. It is the corridor through which supernatural things pass into the natural to become touchable, tangible, and palpable things. It is time for the Church to think.

A person's thinking capacity is limited to the amount and quality of information available to that individual to think about.

Information is the raw material for thoughts; you can only think about what you know, and nobody can think beyond what he knows. So, Paul in his epistle to the Ephesians, prayed: ***"....that they may know".***
What Solomon referred to in *Proverbs 4:23* when he mentioned guarding of the heart, was a mind filled with stuff. Nobody guards an empty house. Solomon believed that an informed mind should be guarded. One of the tricks is not the hijacking of information; it is the corrupting of it. If I draw a dot on a whiteboard and ask anyone around to tell me what they see; no one will say they see a whiteboard. Everyone will talk about the dot; this is because man's attention will always be drawn to marks and mistakes. This is why you can be good to a person for many years only to fall out with them for just one misdeed. At that point, you wonder if they suffer from amnesia. It is because the devil works hard always to corrupt good. Have you ever in the course of eating groundnuts, bit a stone or crushed a bad seed? Some of us get so impatient that we throw everything out; some eat on but not with the same pleasure as they had in the beginning. Your level of faith and fear in a person is dependent on the information available to you to think about. That's why you do some things not knowing they are wrong until someone calls your attention to them. You were not informed enough about that thing. What information is entering your spirit? Jesus told us that freedom is a function of an encounter with truth. He let us know that freedom is not only about the breaking of chains off a man's hands and feet because you can take chains off a man's hands and feet and still have him acting like a slave. After all, his mind is still shackled. ***Free hands and feet don't mean freedom. Every man is limited to the last set of knowledge he/she acquired.***

Some people stopped reading books the moment they wrote their final exams in school; for some that may be around 7 years ago. You are as updated as the last information you acquired.

When you don't think as you should, you easily entertain mediocrity. Mediocrity is a result of stale thinking. There were some things you repelled in the past that now accommodate because you stopped thinking; it is called Gradual Desensitization. How do you feel about an advert on a billboard of a lady dressed half-naked, advertising a refrigerator company? The question you'd be prompted to ask yourself is: “what on earth has a half-dressed woman got to do with home appliances?” How did you feel pornographic content popped up on your screen while you were busy on your computer? You felt bad I presume. The truth is that if you are no longer feeling that way now, you have dropped in thinking. You are accepting it already; that is corruption. The mind is magnetic in nature; things get stuck in it without your knowledge if you are not intentional about censoring what goes in and out of your mind. There are songs you didn't learn but can sing very well because a CD vendor close to you would not stop playing that one song. The first time you heard the song, you protested by raising some worship song but after a while, you realize that while you're driving, you find yourself humming to the songs. After a while, you find yourself compromising your belief because you let the thoughts stay.

There are two kinds of thinkers alive, they are:

1. Survival thinkers, and;
2. Creative thinkers.

The Survival Thinker is the one whose thoughts are largely around: what to eat, what to wear, where to live, and what kind of shoes to buy. This is to a large extent, an unproductive and negative kind of thinking. This is because, while the survival thinker busies himself with these thoughts.

The creative thinker on the other hand, thinks of how to feed others; how to clothe others; how to provide shelter for others; he thinks of real estate; he thinks of manufacturing. Jesus admonished us against survival thinking, referring to people that think that way as gentiles. Some argue that you have to be fed first before thinking of feeding others. I respond to this argument with a simple answer: the man that thinks of how to feed others knows that he can't feed others and goes hungry. The man that thinks of how to manufacture clothes for others knows that he can't do that and go naked. The last thing that the designer of Emporio Armani will be thinking about is a t-shirt to wear because by providing that for millions of people to wear, they have access to millions of t-shirts for themselves. I have never seen a stranded real-estate owner. Move in your thinking. When we got born again, one of those things Jesus did was not to remove our minds.

Transformation is by the renewal of the mind not by the removal of it. When you are praying, engage your mind. Paul said: with the mind, we serve the Lord. One of the major things I've heard while conversing and working with some CEOs as a recruiter is that they wish their staff will think better and take initiative in their work. The best employees are not the ones that toil to impress their bosses the most. The best employees are those who beyond being resourceful for their employers, go on to think up initiatives for themselves and for their employers. They are called intrapreneurs. They are employed but while they are working for their employees, they think of ways to bring about progress to their organization. No matter how bad an economy gets, some people can never go jobless. Some people won't lose sleep when it's time to downsize the staff of their organization because, because of their profitability, they get to downsize with their bosses.

Such people don't get there by sycophancy; they get there by proving to be useful. Profitability is a function of information processed. Ordinary people see problems and complain; exceptional people think up solutions. It is ordinary to complain. Things are not what they should be, undeniably, yes.

So, what are you doing about it in your small sphere of influence? A man who gets a contract to build roads and does not deliver will not do better than he did as a contractor when he becomes a governor. People go to the gym to build and maintain a fit body but seldom do so with their minds. Thinking is to the mind what gym is to the body. **To improve your life, improve your mind.**

Chapter Three

> “
>
> ***if you think only when you're in trouble, then you're in more trouble.***

The Mine's Guide

The truth remains that people think differently and that is why there are obvious differences in our approaches and responses to situations and occurrences, and our varying levels of productivity. A man named Sir Isaac Newton discovered a law that he called the law of gravity; he sat in his orchard and witnessed an apple fall. It was then that the “aha moment” hit him. Then he came up with a question; ***“why don't apples fall upwards?”*** It was based on this question that he discovered the law that has aided man to build so many things. Learn how to see things from an angle that is not obvious. ***Objectivity is genius.***

All the average man would have done had he been there would have been to pick up the apple, thank God for it, and satisfy his appetite. When you walk through your residence area, what do you see, problems or solutions? I want to trigger your thinking. I pray God opens your eyes to solutions; when you see and provide solutions, you will not pray for money. Elementary Economics tells us that money is a reward for service rendered. Pay attention to what you think about. Isaac Newton did not create the law of gravity, he only discovered it. The things we look for are available only waiting for our discovery of them.

Most people only think when they are in trouble; the truth, however, is that if you think only when you're in trouble, then you are in more trouble. A man that prays only when he is in trouble is in serious trouble.

1. Go deep (Think Deep)

Counsel in the heart of a man is like deep waters but a man of understanding will draw it out. -Proverbs 20:5

Oh Lord, how great are your works, your thoughts are deep. -Psalm 92:5

Great thoughts are products of deep thoughts. The wealth of the ocean is never found at the shallow ends, it is always found at its deep ends. Nothing significant is found at the surface. The truth about thinking is that you are either a shallow thinker or a deep thinker. The interesting thing about the mind is that it is flexible; its elastic limit is defined only by its owner. Your mind will always accommodate how you use it. Most of the achievements, advancements, and progress man has made in the world today are products of deep thinking. As a geologist, I realized that most of the precious things we have on the earth are trapped in the crust below us; it takes the daring and the bold to go there and bring them out. Thinking is deep work; it is also hard work, that's why Managers are paid more than the man that mans the gate. Smart work will always pay higher than hard work. Mental exhaustion is more fatiguing than hard labour; mental stress is more critical than physical stress. One day my five-year-old boy came to me and said: dad I'm tired. I asked him what he did that got him tired; he answered that he had been thinking. Because I understood mental stress, I played along and told him to get some sleep. To my amazement, he slept off the moment his body touched the bed. For a while, I kept wondering to myself what he could have been thinking.

People that know this boy, know him to act a little bit older than his age. I wondered why a five-year-old whose fees I pay was mentally exhausted. I seriously cannot wait to see what he will become in the near future. It is as a result of this mental stress that students lose weight on exam day. Some eat more but still lose weight because mental exhaustion does not answer to food; it answers to rest. Leaders are thinkers, and great leaders are deep thinkers. You must be a thinker if you will lead in any sphere of influence. Let your advantage not be grace alone. Let it be an addition to the excellence that you already provide. It was said of Daniel that in matters pertaining to the king and matters of the kingdom he was ten times better than his contemporaries. They found no fault in him until they poked him in the spot he had reserved for his God alone then his God reacted. Don't expect God to react to the things that he expects you to react to. It is time for the church to raise men of cerebral energy whose faith and grace will be found intact. If you are not the best in your organization, the kingdom is not proud of you. How can you have a sound mind and not be producing sound results? The development of your city will begin when you start to think; when you do, the spirit of light will carry what you have imagined. Elijah did not outrun the chariots of Ahab by standing still, he ran. They that wait upon the Lord shall renew their strength; it didn't stop there. The Bible said they shall run. The Lord will take over after you have begun running. Engage your thinking power and he will take over. Go deep, your God is deep. Don't wait for people to masticate stuff and give you food; be the solution provider and let the world benefit from your existence. Your mind will go as far as you push it. It's not about the mind; it's about the man.

Many business owners are struggling because they are trying to solve new challenges with old mindsets.

You'll often find people begin to fall asleep and get distracted when you talk about things that make a man go forward. But this is the core of man. A man that doesn't think will always work for the one that thinks. You know the capacity for deep thinking is always found in children.
If you don't like your current job, then think your way out of it. Get your mind to sweat. Find information with which to think. Wealth does not come to meet anybody at home, your mind reaches for it.

The first thing that affects our depth of thinking is *environmental conditioning.* Our environments will always seek to condition us. It may be quite expensive to get your children to a good school but it is not expensive to create the right thinking environment for them in your house. How you thought as a child was determined by the information that you were exposed to; you didn't have control over it. If as an adult, you are still controlled by what you see then it's your irresponsibility that is to be blamed; you should put away childish things. A lot of us think the way we do right because of conditioning. Some of us were told as children that wealth is only for a selected few. So when a person who was conditioned to believe such grows up, the ideas for wealth that will come to him will always hit a bar in his mind and bounce back because he believes that wealth is only for a selected few.

I have a friend who resigned from his high-paying job to do a lower-paying job just because it challenges his mind. He won't take a job if it doesn't challenge him. If you put a child in a school and the child begins to function on a thought level lower than he was before entering that school, you should consider pulling him out because an inferior level of mental conditioning might be happening to that child. Everyone is born with the ability to go deep into thoughts, we simply lose our curiosity as we grow.

My first time in a sales job, I received a very humongous target and deep within me, I knew that was an impossible target but because I had been conditioned never to say "it can't be done" I accepted the challenge. The sales manager looked at me and asked if I thought the target was realizable, I said "yes we can. He said to me, "and if we can't?" I replied, "We will review it." He turned to me and said, "You think differently". For some people, the response to the second question after bragging would have been, "if we don't then do whatever you think fit for us"; but that's rather repulsive. To my surprise, after the first month, I was like fifteen million down from the target only to exceed it by twenty million the next month. Whatever the mind can grasp, the hand can grab. To become a deep thinker, you have to intentionally position yourself in environments that will spur you on to grow in your thought level. Find people that don't see impossibilities. Do not surround yourself with mediocre; the Bible says that

"He that walketh with wise men shall be wise..." (Proverbs 13:20).

I don't know how it happens but it works. A popular quote says that if you want to be a millionaire, find six millionaires to keep as a company and after a while, you will become the seventh. Run away from people who celebrate mediocrity. If you're already the best in the pack, find another pack. On a scale of one to nine, ten is wonderful but on a scale of one to one hundred, you'll agree with me that ten is nothing. Don't celebrate your wins for too long; get out of the zone and check for deeper waters. That's how some people become principalities and powers where there is no office for a principal because they find it hard to adjust. Get yourself into places where your best is challenged for improvement; most times you will be humbled but stay with the process. Get to travel out of your zone now and then; this will give you another perspective on things.

The next thing that affects how deep a man thinks is exposure. Do all you can to expose your children to a life that is better than yours. While growing up, some of us did not come from wealthy homes but we had inclinations for wealth, so very often, we found ourselves hanging around the children of the wealthy and the wealthy mindset rubbed off on us. Someone told me that while in school, his mother told him not to mingle with rich kids because when trouble sets in, their parents would come for their rescue sooner and faster than his parents would, making it possible for him to die in prison should things go south. The mother advised him to look for kids on the same level as him and be friends with them. This mother didn't realize that something in that child pulled him to a place from whence he can get the whole family out of poverty but the truth is that there is more propensity for a drowning man to pull his savior down with him than there is for him to be saved. It is never too late to get exposure. Never fight exposed people, no matter how little they may appear; do yourself the favor of listening to them for information. Do not put your age before knowledge; fools grow old too. A fool doesn't become wise by growing old; instead, he becomes a foolish old man. In third-world countries, age is deified above wisdom. You will often hear statements like, "listen to your elders"; even when she is ignorant. I will hear her but not listen. Today it has become possible to travel through the internet. Using tools such as Google Maps, you can view any part of the world in real-time. By the time you find out just how tall your favorite skyscraper is. Just then you'll realize that a car is not a luxury. Something will happen to your mind when you visit places like Dubai where the latest Mercedes Benz is used as a taxi. Get yourself to see the sight of car owners who jump the train, not because they can't fuel their cars but because the train can make their journey better. Exposing yourself to such sights will make you lose reverence for those politicians and business people who try to intimidate the ignorant with their Toyota SUVs:

you will understand that car ownership is not a luxury.

My giving life changed after an experience I had in a church in Lagos. I brought out an offering that seemed big to me then, a lady that sat beside me saw what I brought out somehow and asked me if that's all I had to give God. I was still getting immersed in embarrassment when she asked me how much my shoes were worth, and then offered to give me an offering if I didn't have enough. I obliged and without counting, the young lady put her hand in her purse, pulled out some money, and gave it to me. When I counted the sum, it was 30 times what I initially intended to give. I quickly pulled out everything in my pocket and gave it as an offering; after that day, my finances didn't remain the same. Some smart person would have thought it wise to loot the money and give only a portion of what the lady had given them, but something happened to me that day, and my mindset about giving to God changed. I understood that giving is not about "having" it's about "a thinking". For those in the corporate world, when you go out for a buffet with your boss, don't eat, take something light and afterward, go get a meal. Some people don't check your clothes or looks when you're at the table with them, they check out your eating habits. You can borrow everything else to look like who you're not but you can't borrow a self at the dining table.

Give your children a better life than you had; the best way to do this is by exposing them to the knowledge you weren't privileged to have access to while growing up. I remember back then as a child, we were told that children don't eat full boiled eggs. The curious ones among us had to find ways to buy full eggs in secret to know just what was in them. A lot of children start stealing because of the compression of their minds by their parents; they grew to meet the mindset of scarcity prevalent in their environments, so they thought they had to steal to have.

What makes your children not eat when they're out on a visit with you is not the way you look at them. If your child looks at you first before answering a visitor when they're asked by the visitor if they'd have a meal, then you have some mental work to do on them. A lot of our teen girls fall victim to emotional abuse because they didn't hear their fathers say to them for once, “I love you.” So the first time they hear it from a man, it sends a chill down their spine and they start to deify the feeling and the person that made them feel that way to the point of not being able to decipher when the person means well for them and when he doesn't.

When we were young, my father would take my siblings and me to a five-star hotel and bring us back; once he took my little brother and me to an airport and paid for us to get on the plane and see the inside, we didn't fly then. I flew years later but before I did, I was not intimidated by those who would bring reports of their flight experience because I knew that having been on a plane while it was on the ground, it would not take long before I flew in one. My father didn't have much but he made sure that I and my siblings knew that there was more out there than we knew within the house. Expose yourself through books; expose yourself through associations.

The Bible says in Proverbs 27:17 that
“Iron sharpens iron; so a man sharpeneth the countenance of his friend.”

If your friends are not sharpening your countenance, change them. Don't let people choose you as a friend, choose your friends. Don't be friends with anyone that enjoys talking down on others. Mediocre people discuss people; excellent people discuss ideas. This is how to access your friends; ask yourself when last they made you sweat.

Some people do not know that the mind can sweat when it is given a proper portion of thoughts to ponder. There are certain environments you will enter into and you will find out that you are not up to par. Just like Isaiah, you will declare, "I am undone." Isaiah had been prophesying but when he saw the Lord and looked at himself, he realized just how unworthy he was.

Today we have the internet at our disposal; with it, you can travel the world. Bill Gates was exposed to a mainframe computer as a teenager and the result of that exposure is what the whole world benefitted from. At the age of 16 former president of the United States Bill Clinton had the privilege to meet John F. Kennedy to shake his hands; after interacting with the then Head of State, Bill Clinton said to his friends, "one day, I'm gonna have his job." Your current location is not an excuse for mediocrity; you should be competing on a global scale, not on a local level.

That there are no tall skyscrapers where you are is not an excuse for your children not to know that they exist. What you expose them to is a seed; you don't have a guarantee of what the harvest will be. Open their minds to possibilities. Some encounters and experiences would have not let you think and act the way you do if you had met them before now. Conversations and experiences formed the mindsets that made us who we became. A generous man is not the man that has what to give; a generous man is a man with a heart to give. Generosity is not the availability of things; it is a mindset that makes things available with the little one has. Ben Carson's teacher tried to put a limiting mindset in him but his mother changed the narrative. As a parent, take note of what your children listen to; it could do them a lot of harm or it could do them a lot of good. One time in an event where I was invited to speak; a man came to me after observing me for a while and asked me where I come from. I told him I am of Igbo descent. He went on to ask, "Where did you grow up?" I answered, in Enugu State.

He said "but you don't sound like them"; I replied, "Because I exposed myself." The first time I lived outside that city for a long time was during my service year as a core member, but from that place, I exposed myself. I dropped out of school the first time. Upon hearing this, my then business mentor asked me, "You didn't graduate?" I said "no sir". "So what happened then?" I replied to him, "I exposed myself." Education is not gotten in schools, certificates are. Education is a deliberate commitment to knowledge. That's why educational bodies award degrees to men without certificates because although they didn't go to school they show themselves learned enough for certification.

TRADITION: Tradition is another thing that obstructs productive thinking. Tradition will always fight innovation. Naysayer will always tell you, "This is the way it is done." God did not create the mind to be traditional; he made it to be transitional. The paradigms that dominated the past generations have evolved due to the progressive nature of information. Whoever refuses to evolve with the evolving paradigms will be at the back end of innovation. ***"The best way to backslide is to stand at a place where life is moving forward. Once life leaves you behind, you're backslidden".*** "This is the way my father did it" some people tell me but then excuse me, will your father not be confused when you hand him an iPhone? How can you compare your life with your father's? Nobody moves forward on reverse gears.
Making the word of God of none effect through your tradition, which ye have delivered (Mark 7:13) Jesus told the Pharisees. So, even the power of God can be hindered by tradition.
Tradition sometimes makes it hard to challenge the status quo. Progressive climes challenge themselves. You don't just buy into every piece of information passed to you without asking questions; unless your mind is not working. The mind of a man that works is always asking questions. Society makes asking questions look like a crime.

A con man will always be found out when he's asked questions. Do you want answers? Then ask questions. ***We are transformed, not by the removal of our minds but by the renewing of them.***

Chapter Four

> ***The only box there is anywhere, is the one we make up in our minds.***

The Mine Is Boundless

Many times, I've heard people say "think outside the box." If you accept that statement, it means that you believe that there is a box somewhere. The truth however is that there is no box anywhere. Don't tell people to get out of the box, they are in their minds, and not a box. The only box there is anywhere, is the one we make up in our minds. All things are possible with God, the bible says but there is another set of people with whom the bible says there is no impossibility; they that believe.

Note that it didn't say to them that believe in God. So, it's not a matter of whether or not you believe in God, it's a matter of what you believe. Richard Branson of Virgin Galatics has been broken more than twice but every time, he comes back as a multi-millionaire. The billionaire said he believes he cannot be poor. The last time I checked, he's not a believer. My challenge is that believers believe that things are difficult. The city you live in shouldn't box you in, the internet has broken that barrier. One time in Abuja, I realized that people were applying for jobs in Abuja from South Africa, Zimbabwe, Kenya, and other neighboring countries.

70% of people (majority being conservatives) who built sustained businesses built them from nothing. They didn't come from wealthy homes; neither did most of them have rich uncles. They built from the backdrop of poverty. All things are possible to him that believes; don't tell me about where you were born. Your locality is not an excuse. This is what differentiates creative people, innovators, and inventors from everyone else.

Everyone can think but not everybody does. Everyone has a mind that can either expand or compact. The strength of your mind depends on the extent to which you put it to use and not on your labour. Grey matter is grey matter. None is dark grey; all is grey. The mind of a white man is called grey matter; the mind of a black man is still called grey matter. The only change is the color of their skin, not the color of their minds.

We have airplanes today because someone thought man can fly but not just with wings since he didn't have any. Someone thought that a vessel can float on water, no matter the weight of what it carries. When I see ships carrying thousands of containers and still floating by surface tension, I marvel at the creativity of the mind. You are not disadvantaged, no matter what your situation looks like. The Bible says that when your father and mother forsake you, the Lord will pick you up. So, do not think that you are disadvantaged.

Chapter Five

The Mine Is Global

Our environment can condition our minds into being local in our thoughts, manners, and ways. But the onus is on us to decide. If you have shoes on your feet; if you are not walking about naked; if you are reading this book now then it is proof that you are a benefactor of someone's global thought. The saying that the world is a global village is no longer a cliché; it's a reality. I'm sorry to put this to you like this but if you're in business and you haven't thought about selling to the world yet, then you're a victim of the local-thinking conditioning. In modern times, the internet has been able to break the barriers of distance and mistrust between foreign companies and local users through the introduction of more reliable systems such as Blockchain technology.

> ***Imagination builds resolution. Even money responds to a made-up mind.***

The black man believes everywhere that he is marginalized; it's a mindset but BLACK IS NOT DISADVANTAGED. In reality, more blacks are dying at the hands of blacks than at the hands of any other race. You may not have had any power in deciding where you were born but you absolutely have the power to choose where you'll be. The greatest limitations of a man are in his mind.

Now, I want you to do this: Place your right hand on your head and declare this three times, "I cannot be limited; I have the mind of Christ."

You cannot easily destroy a man with a positive mental attitude. Depression most times happens to a man that has difficulty seeing his positive sides. You are only disadvantaged if you say so; everything in life assumes the meaning you give it. So, nothing has any meaning except the meaning you give it. No one can stop the imaginations of a man except that man. Even God agrees with this. Imagination builds resolutions. Even money responds to a made-up mind.

Every resource a man needs to achieve the level of relevance he desires will only respond to him once he makes up his mind. Stop!

Before you continue, make up your mind now that you won't go unnoticed then raise your right hand and say this too; I cannot die unnoticed. I am a global player; I am not a local champion!

It is okay to start local but don't die a local champion. How can you, a believer, die locally? The Holy Ghost you carry is universal, why then should you end local? You are bigger than the grades on your certificate. Wake up every morning and tell yourself, I am a global player. Your current pay should not limit your mind in any way; aim over relevance on a global scale. Do what global players do; read what they read, one day, the world will come looking for you. It is okay to come from a poor background; Jesus Christ came from the same, perhaps a worse background than yours even but it didn't stop him. If you were born in a hospital, you're a king. I imagine Jesus being taunted while he grew up; I imagine folks telling him, "Look, Jesus, stop acting all special; we know you were born in a manger so quit the whole "righteous than thou" thing; you're no better than any of us." This, and maybe worse could they have said to him but nothing said or done to Jesus was able to deter him from his destiny. You are unstable, if only you say so.

All things are possible unto them that believe (Mark 9:23).

Every great thing that happened in the life of Mary began from the moment she said, “Behold the handmaid of the Lord; be it done unto me according to thy word.” Sometimes we receive ideas that seem way bigger than us; at such times, the ideal thing to do would be, “Lord, I am available for whatever you want to do.” Any day you realize that you're only a tool for the actualization of God's purpose on earth, you will go far. No arrow shoots itself. You are an arrow in the hand of God, and the archer in whose hand you're in is very precise. When the idea comes, jump on it and believe it with every might within you.

You may not look like a global phenomenon now but it's only a matter of time before you become it as long as you fix your thoughts on it. Do not let yourself deviate to start thinking subsistence; keep your mind on global relevance and work on your thoughts. Don't allow traditions to keep you down. People with global visions will always have a lot of destinies dependent upon their rising. Rise, the world is waiting for you.

Chapter Six

> ***Big achievement is a product of big thinking. You cannot think "I can't" and can.***

The Mine Is More

To think big is to have the ability to do big. You can't think small and do big things. A lot of people will not be able to do big things because the container they provided for the possibilities cannot contain the resources that will come for the achievement of those possibilities. The container is the mind; you can only carry as much as your mind can contain. Many people expect 500 liters of resources whereas their minds are only about 7 liters large. If you're given a hundred million for a startup and your mental capacity is only 5 million, it's only a matter of time before the money comes down to what your mind can carry. If your parents were meager thinkers, there is every possibility that you'll be one too (if you are not already) unless you commit to intentionally making yourself a mega thinker.

If your children will not see the world as small, then be sure to make sure that they never think that the world is small. I grew up thinking that my father can do anything. I also have taken it upon myself to make sure my children believe the same about me; so many times, my little boys come to me and ask, "Daddy, can you kill a lion?"

My answer to them when they come up with these questions is usually, “Yes”. “Daddy can you kill Goliath of the Bible?” They would ask me; “oh yes you bet I can.” is what I reply to them every time. “David was a young boy and he was able to kill him right?” I'd ask them; “Yes.” “Am I a small boy?” They'd say no; “then I can kill him” I reply.

I am intentionally forming a thought pattern in their head. One day, I went to pick them up from school and I overheard them saying to their peers; “My dad can buy anything, except the things he does not want to buy.” As long as those boys are concerned, there's nothing I can't buy; so what I do after hearing them say that is that whenever they come to me asking for anything, I tell them to go and pray to God, telling Him to provide money so that I can buy them what they want. I do this to intentionally move their mind away from me, and put their trust in the sufficiency of God instead of mine because I understand that I am limited. I make them see God as the provider of all things while I project myself to them as merely being a channel.

Big achievement is a product of big thinking. You cannot think “I can't” and can. Make sure that your inner conviction is in tandem with your external hustle. If they don't agree, then you're wasting your time. A lot of people that traveled abroad and made it did so because they formed a conviction in their minds that they'd become successful once they travel abroad. Some didn't even have any plans but what they did to become successful is inconsequential compared to the conviction that drove them in the first place.

Results are premised on efforts, and efforts are products of thoughts. To think big is to think in large sizes; huge sizes are however relative. The same one million that may appear large to someone may be of less value to someone else.

The mind of a man can think big and it can think small depending on the user. Every new idea has a larger and broader version of it. You can only think to the extent to which you have expanded your mind. A simple test would be to ask two people to draw up a business plan for a restaurant; you will be shocked to see the quality of both minds on paper. One time, we were building a space for our local church and one day at the site, a man walked up to me to inquire if the place would be our permanent site or not. I told him it was only a temporary space and he screamed; "Why then are you doing all these as if it's your father's land" he asked. "Why don't you just put up a minor structure with zincs?" At this point, I had to answer him; "I am building a structure where I can worship my God; it's not a permanent structure but my God does not dwell in hot environments; maybe your God does but mine does not." If you must be a high achiever, then big thinking must be a habit. Don't wait to be pushed before you think. If you can afford it, don't raise your children in a small house.

If you cannot, then make it a habit to always take them out to where they'll find big spaces; it affects how they turn out in the future. Challenge yourself always to think big. Sometimes, breakthrough is not money in the bank; sometimes, it's breaking into a new horizon of thinking. If you've never boarded a plane before, please gather money and do so. You may be surprised to see this if you've been flying all your life but the truth is that there are people who have never been inside a plane all their lives. The boundaries of your mind can always be stretched to new limits, provided you're ready to learn. If you dream of owning a car, get up and go to a dealer near you; ask questions about the functionality of the car of your choice, and go home. It does something to your mind. All these are ways to shift the way you think. You cannot attract what you don't know.

Don't be your own prayer point; if you can think it, don't stop thinking. A lot of people get ideas and the first thing that crosses their minds is how much they have in their bank accounts. ***Every vision comes with a vision; just give it an allowance.***

I made up my mind a long time ago not to argue with people with low thinking because I found out that most times, they rarely understand a thing you say, leaving you frustrated, angry, and almost pissed with them. The truth is that your being pissed with them does not reset their thought pattern in any way so, the best thing is to simply avoid such people. There's an old wise saying that says that a man that does not know and does not know that he does not know is a fool, but the bigger fool is the one that does not know and does not want to know that he does not know. Small thoughts are the outputs of a mind trained by installed limitations, fear, and disappointments; anyone with such a mindset has to intentionally break out of it. Don't argue when you find out that this is your case, be open to growth and adjustment. Some very spiritual people, so to say, have issues with accepting this. Most times, God answers our prayers but lack of exposure keeps us backward.

A lot of people hinder their blessings by their actions which are reflections of their thought level. A man that thinks big will always act big. No one is born a winner, and no one is born a loser; we are all born choosers. Whether you'll be a small thinker or a big thinker; it's your choice. In 1899 a man called Charles H. Duell, the then commissioner of the US patent office was quoted to have said that everything that can be invented had been invented. I imagine what he would do if he were here to find out that we now have little devices in our hands with which we can talk to someone continents away from us without having to shout.

The problem with most people who think small is that they are too often repellent to new knowledge; they are always not willing to learn.

Some people get into a discussion that they know little or nothing about and they never keep calm to learn from others. Keeping quiet is a skill that learners know how to use very well. Resist the urge to claim a level that you have not attained. People miss their helpers that way; may the man that was sent to help you not meet you with a car you borrowed. What that means is that you should not borrow to keep up with a level that you have not yet attained. One time, I was led to give someone one of my pairs of shoes, and I saw a very expensive shoe on his feet. I admired the shoe and commended the shoe; he responded that the shoe was one of the many such brought to him from overseas by one of his brothers. So, I felt like I had been misled until one day I overheard some people talking about the same young man and his borrowing lifestyle. I called him and asked him then he told me that it was just so he could be packaged.

One of the reasons why people settle for small thinking is so they won't be tagged failures. For some, it's because of past failures. So they avoid anything that will make them stretch their minds beyond their comfort zones.

One of the most effective ways to change your paradigm is by association. Find big thinkers and make them your friends.

Chapter Seven

> ***The rate of transformation in a man's life is directly proportional to the rate of renewing that his mind has been subjected to.***

The Mine of Possibilities

In a world filled with pessimists, differentiate yourself by being optimistic. Pessimism is defined as the tendency to see the worst aspect of things or a strong belief that the worst will happen. Oftentimes, pessimists are known to never see good in anything. You'll share an idea with them and usually, the only thing they can tell you is how the idea will not work. Pessimism has never birthed any new thing; optimism on the other hand has always done the opposite. Optimism is the belief, confidence, or conviction that something will go well. When I wanted to go back to school, a business mentor told me that I was too old to go back to school; that I should focus on my business; or take an evening class, part-time, or something. I went ahead with my plans, however, despite his attempts to dissuade me. At graduation, I went back to him and showed him my results; I was the best graduating student in my class. When he saw the result, he exclaimed, "Wow. I knew you'd make it."

No child born into this world was born with a pessimistic mindset; we are all born with optimism.

As we grow up sadly, some people get conditioned by their environments to become pessimistic in thinking. The many discouragements, dissuasions and all became factors that formed very strong pessimistic walls within them. Those times you wanted to attempt a jump and someone by the side told you, “No, you can't achieve that.” Those times you wanted to run and they told you can't. All the “You cants” make you very pessimistic, and sadly, now that you're grown, you're still very scared to dare anything or to even take risks; your mind interprets risk as a failure. There is nobody that broke forth that didn't do so by taking risks. Life answers to the bold. Everything that has been created was created by optimistic minds. The best way to develop this kind of thinking is to surround yourself with people that believe that nothing is beyond reach; everything is **takeable.**

He that walks with the wise, the Bible says, shall himself be wise (Proverbs 13:20).

The rate of transformation in a man's life is directly proportional to the rate of renewing that his mind has been subjected to. This is how it works friend; **Change your mind; change your life.**

Beloved, I wish above all things that you prosper and be in good health even as your soul prospers. 3 John 2

It is the prosperity of your mind first that determines the prosperity of your body and your hands. A truly wealthy mind is prosperous first in his mind. You can't be poor in your mind and be prosperous in your hands. Visible wealth and success are created by invincible things.

.....so that the things which are seen were not made from things which do appear. (Heb 11:3).

The true worth of a man is in the quality of his mind. Henry Ford built his first car without reverse; he was mocked but he went back and rebuilt it. Today, Ford is one of the best car makers around. He was asked one time what he would do if he lost all his wealth, and he answered that his wealth is more than what can be seen on the outside. "You can take my factories, burn up my buildings, but give me my people and I'll build the business right back again." For some people, their parents chose their mindsets for them but the good news is that you can choose again. A truly wealthy person is free from fear and doubt. Anyone that has conquered doubt has conquered failure.
Now I want you to raise your right hand and declare this believing every single word in it; **IT WILL WORK OUT FOR MY GOOD!**

Don't say it if you don't believe what you're saying. The largest part of a man's wealth is his positive mental attitude. Wake up every morning and expect the best. Never allow the inner voice to tell you that you're disadvantaged; you are not. A healthy mind gives birth to a healthy body, a healthy pocket, and healthy relationships. The best way to predict a bright future is to create it; the best way to create is to take control of your mind.

Finally brethren, whatsoever things are true, whatsoever things are honest, whatsoever things are just, whatsoever things are pure, whatsoever things are lovely, whatsoever things are of good report: if there be any virtue and if there be any praise, think on these things. Philippians 4:8

You decide where your mind goes. This power to decide however comes from what you ponder on. What do you think about?

Chapter Eight

> ***It is unwise to think of the future as being in the future because the future has already begun.***

The Mine Has Posterity

A very popular cliché declares that the youths are leaders of tomorrow. As good sounding as this is, it is one of the greatest lies ever told to the young. This deception makes the youth think that the future is ahead of them; what they do not know is that today is the future; they talked about yesterday in expectation. What we call tomorrow when we get to it, will not look like tomorrow; it will still look like today. We must, at every time, fight to use the resources at our disposal to create the desired future for ourselves that is desirable. The best way to predict your future is to create it. The future is actually a mirage because the future we now live in is largely the output of how we handled our today. So, what we call the future is not about to come; it is what we are already building with bricks of the moments in our present. Where we are today is greatly influenced by the decisions we made in the past, and where we'll be tomorrow will be largely determined by the decisions we are making now. The decisions we make at the junctions of life when acted upon with discipline are the factors of life that will eventually determine our outcomes tomorrow or what we know as the future. It is unwise to think of the future as being in the future because the future has already begun.

This is why procrastination is deadly: it puts your life on pause when life is in motion. Our results are products of our actions and our actions are products of our decisions, and our decisions are products of our thoughts. If you must have the right results in what you call the future then you must think right now. Many great organizations folded up at the demise of their founders; they didn't understand this truth. The man was waiting for the future to come before making plans for the future. You don't wait for the future to come to make plans for the future; you make plans for the future today. There are things you said you'll do at 25 that you remembered when you clocked 27. You had the nudge to do it then but you said you were still young. The worst mistake a young person can make is to believe that he is still young. The decisions of destiny are not taken when you mature; they are taken when you come into awareness. Maturity is a mirage. It is not a function of age; it is a product of awareness and exposure. What people refer to as their future is what someone else is already living in, so it is foolish to define your future by another person's timeline.

How you think in the present, always affects your future. Most people fail to realize this until they are living in the future. It happened to us in college; some of us believed that the first and second years were times for fun. Only to realize in the first semester of the third year, that you have wasted years. They didn't know that their futures began to count from the time they set foot in college. The key to achieving your desired result for tomorrow is INTENTIONALITY. Intentional and deliberate actions taken toward your desired end are what prepare you for the future you hope for. How prepared are you?

In thinking about the future, consider the following perspectives;

SPIRITUAL AND PERSONAL GROWTH: Growth is an intentional feat. Growing old, we cannot handle but growing old is deliberate. The truth is that a seed that is not planted cannot grow. The illusion of spiritual men is that they think that life rides, and is driven by miracles. It is a bastardization of grace to think that grace happens by chance. Grace works better with intentionality. What you do today about your personal growth is what will make your life not be prayer points when you get to the place you are praying for. Many people realized very late that irresponsibility never pays well.

They get to very tight corners and start expecting God the all-powerful to step in for them. You can't sow irresponsibility as a seed and expect a good life. Your personal and spiritual development is dependent on your commitment to activities that sponsor growth in these areas.

Commitment strengthens your capacity to commune and connect deeper with God, and also your capacity to achieve more. Unfortunately, commitment is one of the many words that this generation of young people does not want to hear. We live in the days when mentees are busier than their mentors. The days where mentees fix appointments with their mentors and do not show up nor even call to explain why they couldn't keep to the appointment; and when asked to give reasons for their absence, they tell you that they were busy. When you want a thing so bad, you go for it; you don't sit and wait for it to come to you. If God gives you a mentor that has the heart of God, hold him with all your heart.

A rolling stone does not gather moss. I remember being told by my father when I was younger that no seed grows by running around; if a seed will grow, then it must allow itself to be subjected to the process of planting, which in turn, guarantees its growth.

It will age but it won't grow. Aging is mandatory; growth is optional. What plans do you have for the future? I hear people say, "I trust the will of God; wherever God takes me to; whatever He tells me to do."

The truth is that one of the major factors that guarantee your lifting in life is diligence. We easily procrastinate personal and spiritual growth because we think we don't need them for our day-to-day routine. You may not consider them of much importance to you in your day-to-day routine but your investment in them plays a major role in your significance. The presence of God is not a gift. It is a reward for a rich fellowship life with the spirit of God. Don't be like Samson that said, I will appear like other times. It is a reward for constant fellowship. A very easy way to prove this is to place two believers side by side and ask them to say, "Praise The Lord." The result is that the effect will not be the same for the two people. The presence of God is different from anointing. Anointing is a special, endowed grace of God upon a man; it can come and go. A may not be anointed but have an anointed voice; a man that carries the presence on the other hand does not need to sing.

He walks into a place and you can easily detect that there is something about him. The result of consistent fellowship pays off over time. 15 years from now, will men be able to detect the elevation point in your life. I hear people pray and tell God that they want to work in the United Nations, and serve in the political sector without any cerebral capacity. If you want to really serve in such a capacity then you must know that it doesn't happen by prayer alone. There is a requisite level of cerebral and social growth you must attain to be able to achieve this.

CAREER GROWTH: The tragedy of 9-5 is that people plan their life in a 30-day routine; so before the 27th day of the month, they already ran out of cash, and life becomes miserable again.

They continue in this cycle and if they fail to realize and do something about it on time, they end up frustrated in the long run. A lot of people see their career as a means of livelihood; most times, career people live off credits. Some wear, drive and live in houses they haven't paid for. An unfortunate web of importunity. Cut your coat according to the resources available and not according to your size. Too many people are stuck with jobs that they don't like because they don't have what it takes to do the job that they like. People are stuck doing things they have never loved doing because they initially didn't think about the future. What are you doing towards the future that you desire? What are your plans? The way to a glorious future is always tarred with two things; one commitment, the other determination. You need determination because the resources available to you for commitment are not enough. I have met people who came to me asking me for tuition fees because they used their tuition money to purchase shoes.

How can you be looking for money to purchase the form for a professional exam and you are using a phone that is worth triple the amount for that form? This generation is more impression-oriented than they are impact-oriented. That's why opportunists make good money from them. Imagine a student who didn't prepare for exams praying to God to remind them of what they didn't prepare for. The Holy Ghost brings things to our remembrance but not nonexistent things. What will he bring to your remembrance if he gets into your knowledge bank and finds it empty?

A generation where jobless people go about with 3 phones in their possession; one of which is worth about the same amount of money they need as capital for a business start-up. Now speaking of the old, I was rather devastated when a young man who came to me for assistance with his tuition some time ago said that his mother had told him that the available money with her then was money she was saving for the burial of her deceased mother.

The befitting burial of this woman's dead mother was a more important cause to her than the future of her child. The young man in question was on his side trying to show me why I should consider helping him. A worthy reason indeed. God gave me the heart to help but he also gave me a mind not to condone irresponsibility and foolishness. I was hard on the young man, who had the nerve to present his mother's reason for not meeting up with her responsibility instead of convincing his mother about her foolish choice. My Consultancy work as a priest has exposed me to all sorts of people with their varying kinds of foolishness.

PHYSICAL AND SOCIAL ENVIRONMENT: Great things don't happen to people because they are growing older. You are not entitled to greatness simply because you are growing old. Things don't become well because you grew old. What kind of life do you want for your future self? Where would you want to live? What kind of life do you desire for yourself and your family? Can your present way of life acquire you that desired place and position over time, should you continue in it? Some years back, I worked in the same office with a young man who told me that he wanted to build a company. This young man was a chronic late-comer who thought entrepreneurship would afford him time to live as he wanted. He didn't know that people will always handle their things the exact way they handle that which belongs to others. Back then, we were always making deductions from his salary as a penalty for late-coming. So, most times, he went home with just 65% of his earnings because the other part was going to penal fees. One day, he called me and asked if I wished him luck as he had just started his firm. Six months later, he found out just how easy it is to be an entrepreneur.

Diligence does not pay your neighbor; diligence pays you. Of diligence, the Bible says, “Seest thou a man diligent in his business…..” That informs you that finding diligent people is not an easy task. In our society today, we refer to people who are shrewd in their business as wicked people because they don't take irresponsibility lightly; because they don't joke with accountability. As for our dear friend, he went looking for a job shortly after our conversation. If you cannot control that which is another man's, you will lose control of yours; the young man learned this the hard way. A lot of times, because they don't find it hard to say, “NO.” More people have gotten into trouble because they couldn't say, “no.”

YOUR HEALTH: It is possible to live a healthy long life. Obedience and adherence to the principles that make for a healthy life make that possible. Healthy living is a product of intentionality. Most times, people fall victim to the brute blows of nature due to negligence and carelessness. Our eating, sleeping, and exercise habits all contribute to our overall physical well-being. One time, I went to a conference with a few brethren, and as we prepared, I told them to prepare well against cold; one of them said to me, “I have eternal life, I can handle cold.” A few days into the conference, we saved this brother from catching pneumonia. A lot of times, as our body systems differ, our bodies don't react the same way when exposed to certain conditions. Living in divine health is a function of divine wisdom and intentionality. Wearing a glass does not reduce the spirituality of the man who uses it to aid his sight. Medicine and its practitioners are gifts from God.

Family: When I counsel young people on relationships, I always ask them, “What kind of man/woman do you want to marry?” My father once said to me, if you wish to know how your wife will look when she is old, look at her mother.

The will of God is not always short, ugly, and not well-to-do.The will of God can be fine, fair, lovely, and well to do too. Many people marry for the interest of their business and end up having frustrating experiences in marriage. Many pastors confuse their youths with the will of God; not so. I don't choose the will of God for people. They bring the will of God and I confirm for them. A lot of people don't consider the future of their children when making marital choices. The one who will be busy with business does not know that he will need a homemaker to take care of the affairs at home when he's away. If you're not always around as a man, know that your children will take after your wife's mindset; until of course, they can make choices for themselves. Your choice of spouse is a testament to the way you think.

WEALTH: Where do you see your finances in the future? In what category will you fall into in the future of wealth? Do you see yourself becoming a person of wealth in the coming days? No need to look far for the answer to these questions; just look at your current financial habits. Do they depict brightness in your economical future? There are no two sides to this coin; no one is wealthy by chance. Your current pattern of thoughts and financial thought-lines can be used to predict your financial future. Every wealthy person first became wealthy in their thoughts. You will naturally grow into whatever picture your mind has drawn for your future. To brighten this picture, you must intentionally choose your line of thoughts and actions, making sure that they tally with what you see in your mind.

In all your thinking, make sure that you put your future into consideration. Be involved in people's affairs. Show up for people when they need people because you will always reap what you sow.

Your choice of friends also forms the environment that conditions your thoughts. Wood will never sharpen iron; intentionally choose relationships that position you for healthy thinking; remember, as a man thinketh, so is he.

Paul let us know that there is a pathway to thinking; there is how to think (Philippians 4:8). If you don't think, you will stink. It's time to think! Believers don't think. How can you believe that a witch can stop the vision that God gave you? If you think well, you'll realize that the source of a thing is the sustenance of that thing. How can the devil destroy what God gave you? Have you realized that witches don't always attack people in Five-star hotels? Sometimes to be delivered from a witch you don't need prayer. There are two ways to change the environment; it's either you move to that environment where they don't have access or you make your environment look like it. Your condition is not as bad; stop trying to attract pity. Once I saw a post on social media of a man without hands giving money to a beggar, and the post was captioned, "Condition is in the mind." I started taking care of myself when I was 17; I left my father's house finally at the age of 22. For 18 months, my mother would not talk to me because I left her house; well, I didn't mind.

Today she's very happy that I left. One of the major things that cripple mental productivity, especially in our days is the comfort zone. Late Dr. Ubong King of blessed memory (bless his soul), said to me, "Divine, hunger is a blessing. Hunger will make you think. When you have to go home to nothing because you have none to cook for you and you know you left nothing at home, you will think." Some people are lousy because at 28, and 38, they are still in their father's house, and they still dare to ask their parents why there is no food in the house. Is what you have in your head cotton wool? The comfort zone makes people mentally lazy; it keeps them comatose.

The worst thing that will happen to you is to have someone who is always giving you something; if you're not intentional enough, your mind will be conditioned to depend on it. The help you are looking for is not outside; it's inside you. Man needed help, God seeing that it was not good for him to be alone, reached into man and created help for man out of what he made man with, provided a woman for man, and called her help. It's a principle in scripture that everything you call help is attracted by what you have on your inside. They told you there's a generational curse on your family, and you believed? Who cursed you? ***The Blessing was here before the curse; the blessing is older than the curse.***

Think your way out of poverty. If as a woman, you only know how to open your legs to men, it is because you don't know how to open your head. When you open your head, you will have reasons to close your legs. Marriage is not a poverty alleviation program; it is the joining of a man and his wife. What most ladies fail to see is that you don't become a wife when you're married; you get married because you are a wife.
It is he that findeth a wife. By implication, that means you are a wife before you are found (Proverbs 18:22).

Who then is a wife? A wife is a caretaker. If you don't already have something you are taking care of, you can't take care of a man. This is one of the main reasons why divorce rates are soaring these days. Boys are marrying women who are not responsible enough to take care of anything.

Chapter Nine

”

Objectivity is a product of intentional thinking.

Garbage In The Mine

Almost every man desire to achieve great results. There's that inward craving to have and attain great feats, yet it is not a thing of desire. Desire on its own is only as strong as running tap water, able to wash off a few stains here and there but never able to move a foot. Desire must be empowered by deliberate actions for it to yield desirable outcomes. The desire for success and good life must be accompanied by intentional efforts because, in the mine, there's garbage loitered all over. Existing to obstruct and veil the treasures in the mine, here are some of the garbage you'll find in the mine as you set out to break out of the box:

CONVENTIONS: Deliberately deliver yourself from conventional thinking; that's the path to innovation. Conventional thinking simply refers to a pattern or method of doing something established over some time to be accurate and almost absolute at times. It is the way your immediate environment processes and interprets matters.

One time at an event, while the attendees were being refreshed, the ushers got to a nicely-dressed man whom I knew to be successful and told him that they had run out of his choice of meal.

Immediately, the man got upset. This man could afford to host everyone in that event but he got upset because he thought he was being marginalized. I was disappointed at him; instead of thinking that, he could've easily redirected his thoughts to think something else; perhaps, who knew? Maybe he didn't get to have that meal because he was better than everyone else who did. But then, he didn't see it that way. When you think freely, you will not react to matters, you will respond. Objectivity is a product of intentional thinking.

Conventional thinking is usually masked in this statement, "This is not the way it is done". Always ask yourself, "Is there any other way to do this?" That's how ideas come. Today, people are coming up with very creative ways to propose to a lady because we got thinking. The old method of ring-in-the-ice-cream-cup is now cliché because a lot of ladies swallowed their rings and didn't even realize it. **Genius begins with questioning the conventional. A man that fights change never changes.**

Never fight what you do not understand; bend down and learn. You cannot produce new results with old strategies. The prosperity you seek is in your mind, and not on the streets. Don't be moribund in your thinking. You can't have a better family than your parents did if you choose to marry your spouse the same way that your parents married themselves.

Now, here's a little exercise for you. Read the statement below and declare it loudly to yourself;

I AM BORN TO BREAK TRADITIONS

SITUATIONS: Besides traditions and conventions, the next thing in the way of innovative thinking is SITUATION. The situations and circumstances that we find ourselves in many times are innovation killers. Certain situations fight and resist creativity in many ways, of pleasant and unpleasant situations, the one that frustrates innovative thinking the most is pleasant situations. Pleasant situations create zones called comfort zones. More men and inventions have died in their comfort zone than anywhere else. Many would-be-successful entrepreneurs are not achieving their full potential because someone is paying them an allowance of a hundred and fifty thousand dollars monthly. Another man with a big industry idea is wallowing away in an oil company where his needs are being well taken care of. Everyone talks about how much footballers make, but only very few think about the men that pay these footballers.

A boy-hawker was approached by a man who offered to buy everything on his tray, and while he made the package ready, a conversation ensued between him and his customer. The man asked him why he was not in school and he told him. Again the boy reminded the man that he wouldn't be able to finish everything on his tray; then, the man told him that he was buying the fruits for his nephews and niece. The young boy let his mouth go wide open in amazement, and the man asked him, you're probably wishing you were one of my nephews and nieces right?

" The young boy replied, "No. I'm thinking of becoming like you when I grow. Then I can buy for my nephews and nieces too, just like you've done." When he said this, the man who was now stunned at the little boy's mind requested to be taken to his parents for talks on how to get the little boy back to school. When they got to the boy's parents, the man offered to take the boy with him but the boy refused; he said to the man, "You can sponsor me but I'll stay with my mother.

The table and trays don't belong to me, they belong to my mother but I don't want my mother in the sun. I'll stay with her."

The young boy didn't let his situation condition the way he thought. He understood that it was only a situation and not a destination. You can be anything in life. Anything!!! You have no excuse to fail in life. I promised myself that I will always be the giver wherever I find myself; whether in cash or kind. So, it doesn't matter whether you meet cash on me or not, I am always ready to give and make sure that no one passes by me who remains the same. If you can't build people up, don't tear them down.

You can become anything you think you condition your mind to think of. I don't look like a school dropout even though I did drop out of school one time. But I told myself that I won't remain on the floor; it's called "A Bounce-back Mindset." The righteous the bible says, fall seven times. The number seven was not used there for enumeration purposes; it was used to depict perfection. In other words, the righteous fall perfectly. So perfectly, every chance of him getting back up is ruled out. Don't allow any situation to keep you down; always think victory. I wish that all women would think like Iya Alakija of Lagos; this will let them know that they are not just here to have babies. Don't go through stuff and come out smelling like it; go through the fire but don't smell smoke. Go through and come out wearing cologne.

Deliver yourself from the pity party, do the party. Some people intentionally wear rags so that the unsuspecting would pity them, now that's a bad way to live. Every day is a beautiful day. I tell people around me never to carry themselves about as people in need of a pity party.
You never know who you're going to meet at any point in time when you're not on guard. **Never be caught un-fresh.**

Don't say I don't have. You may not have it yet but if you think you can have it, then you will. So, when people ask you about a thing, just tell them, **"I DON'T HAVE IT YET."** Don't miss adding the **"YET"**. It shows that you're on your way. Don't put a stop where life put a coma. Bob Marley said emancipate yourself from mental slavery for none but ourselves can free our minds. Deliverance does not come from the external, it comes from within us. It is time to think. If you are challenged, don't feel bad. Only backward people feel bad when they are challenged. Light will determine what you see but your mind determines how you see it.

Now say this too, **"MY MIND IS HEALTHY, I AM UNSTOPPABLE."**

This statement is true if you believe it about yourself. Many of the great achievers you admire today were in worse places than you are now when they started.

Chapter Ten

> ”
>
> ***Your natural habitat is your place of grace.***

The Mine Explorer

Creativity flourishes more when a man is in his natural habitat. Your natural habitat is the only place you can be a star. It is the only place you can be appreciated, celebrated, and rewarded. Once I saw a picture of Lionel Messi in a basketball jersey; some person said he has conquered football and therefore thought it wise to have him try basketball. The moment I saw that picture, I knew Messi would not do so well as a basketball because football is his natural habitat. I noticed something about us Africans (it was done to me too). Once we notice that a child is doing well in a particular area of education, we ignore that area and pay attention to the areas he's not doing well. Take a child who is good at Geography for instance; once we notice that the same child is not so good with Mathematics, we ignore Geography and pay attention to Mathematics. We even go further to get the child tutors who would help them become better at Mathematics instead of getting them a Geography tutor to get them to be exceptional at Geography.

Just then, the child puts all his efforts into trying to learn Mathematics and ends up being an average student.

Some people get depressed on Sunday night because they have to be at their jobs on Monday morning; and on Friday evenings, they are happiest. This is a sign that such a person is not in his/her natural habitat. A man that stays up all night on some work and does not get tired is in his natural habitat. The Lion is the king of the jungle but that same Lion that is king in the jungle will be a victim in the ocean. No matter how you teach a Lion to swim, it can never be king in the ocean because it is not in it to be in the ocean. We are taught to find where the money is going and pursue it. As good as this statement looks; it's not the total truth. The best money you can eat in life is the money you make enjoying yourself; doing what you like to do. The question now is: What is your natural habitat?

It is labour to think when you're outside your natural habitat and very exciting to think in your natural habitat; very exciting. Some time ago, I watched a video on Youtube where the renowned gospel music artiste Micah Stampley gave a young boy his microphone to do some vocal stunts; they both had phones as they did. While I was watching this, a friend said to me: these people are being paid for having fun and enjoying themselves. You can only be a king in the place of your natural habitat because there, you can think through.

HOW DO YOU IDENTIFY YOUR NATURAL HABITAT?

Your natural habitat is in that which you love doing. You don't need to pay me to speak. I will be there talking already before you even invite me for an official speaking event. So, I can study all night and still be up at 6 am because I enjoy doing it. When I met my wife, I kept giving her book gifts until she protested saying: I can never read like you; allow me to be myself. Some people love to draw, they can stay up all night drawing; give them one page of a book to read and they doze off after the first three lines. Why will you push such a person to be a doctor?

Please do not push your children to be what you were not able to be. I have a doctor friend who will always be moody once he's on call but his best becomes very visible whenever he's decorating. He's the best Interior and Exterior decorator in South Eastern Nigeria. He can be on his feet for 4 days making sure a place looks good. According to him, he gets design inspiration even from dreams.

Your thinking prowess comes out effortlessly when you're in your natural habitat. Your natural habitat is your place of grace. It is God's job to bring you into an experience but it is your job to explore and find out for yourself what's in the experience for you. Some people cannot do business no matter what you do to them. If they learn it, they will be able to do it but they will not be fulfilled. That one thing you get fulfillment from doing; that's your natural habitat. There are people in banks who are gifted teachers. Consultancy is teaching too. If you can teach, what are you doing in a bank chasing targets? That's why they stay up all night asking God when it will end. It will not end until you end it. The difference is going to be that instead of writing statements to companies, you will be writing proposals to them on how to train their staff. I am not a white-collar job but whatever you do, create time every day to think about what you were born to do. While you are working in that office to keep body and soul together, think daily about what you were born to do and make sure that your world hears you before you die.

I must work the works of him that sent me while it is day: night cometh when no man can work (John 9:4)

Don't die on the job. Some people say that JOB means Just Over Broke. Well, it may not be all true but don't die without finding your assignment. Your assessment in life is based on your assignment.

Don't copy the behavior and customs of this world, but let God transform you into a new person by changing the way you think. Then you will learn to know God's will for you, which is good and pleasing and perfect. Rom 12:2 NLT

As I studied this scripture, I realized that the will of God is from His mind. So, the renewing of a man's mind makes him think the way God does. He begins to take decisions as God would, and act as God would. However, this is only possible when man's mind has been subjected to renewal by the word of God. A popular thought suggests that logos is used to describe the written word but that's not all of it. The Greek word is used to describe the thoughts of a man. When the word logos was used in the Bible to describe God's word, it is referring to God's thoughts. The raw material for getting your mind to function as God's mind does is the Bible, God's penned-down thoughts. It was written to be spoken and it was spoken to be written. As you read and study the written word, it can change how you think.

If you can change how you think, you will be able to change your reality. There's no limit to how far you can think. If God's wish is that we think the way he does, then it is important to understand that God's thought pattern is the highest there is. If you wish to know how He thinks, then look around you; the world you see and live in, and the ones you do not see are portraits of God's thought pattern. There is a postulation that says that God created the world out of nothing. Looking at the Bible critically, I have a premise upon which to conclude that this postulation is incorrect.

The Bible says that after God created the things he created, He looked at each of them and concluded that they are good. That tells me that there was a comparison; if there is not a replica then there would be no comparison. The Bible says that he looked at Light after making it and saw that it was good; it could not have been good if he didn't have an idea of what good should look like. An architect most times does not need to look at the plan on paper to see if the building is what he wants it to look like because the plan was first in his head before it came on paper. He lives in the house first before everyone else meets the physical building. When he comes to the construction site and after observing what's being done, comments, "good work", he says that it's not because the engineer made the mortar perfectly. The statement is a result of his satisfaction with the engineer's ability to transport what was envisioned and put on paper, from paper to reality.

When God finished making you, he looked at you and said, "This is good." He compared you with what He had in mind and said that. A lot of things try to engineer our minds into boxes that are not there. Don't be your own prayer point. Sometimes, ideas hit you and the first thing you do is try to box them into the scarcity that your mind puts there. The money you're looking for is in your mind.

www.ingramcontent.com/pod-product-compliance
Lightning Source LLC
LaVergne TN
LVHW090133160826
845673LV00017B/2459

* 9 7 8 9 7 8 7 8 1 4 6 7 3 *